THE ULTIMATE
WOOD-FIRED OVEN
BOOK

REVISED & EXPANDED 2nd EDITION

ANNA CARPENTER

Schiffer Publishing Ltd

4880 Lower Valley Road • Atglen, PA 19310

Other Schiffer Books on Related Subjects:
Dutch Oven: Cast-Iron Cooking Over an Open Fire.
Carsten Bothe. ISBN: 9780764342189. $29.99

PUBLISHED BY SCHIFFER PUBLISHING, LTD.
4880 LOWER VALLEY ROAD
ATGLEN, PA 19310
PHONE: (610) 593-1777; FAX: (610) 593-2002
E-MAIL: INFO@SCHIFFERBOOKS.COM

For the largest selection of fine reference books on this and related subjects, please visit our website at
www.schifferbooks.com.
You may also write for a free catalog.

This book may be purchased from the publisher.
Please try your bookstore first.

We are always looking for people to write books on new and related subjects. If you have an idea for a book, please contact us at
proposals@schifferbooks.com

Schiffer Books are available at special discounts for bulk purchases for sales promotions or premiums. Special editions, including personalized covers, corporate imprints, and excerpts can be created in large quantities for special needs. For more information contact the publisher.

In Europe, Schiffer books are distributed by
Bushwood Books
6 Marksbury Ave.
Kew Gardens
Surrey TW9 4JF England
Phone: 44 (0) 20 8392 8585; Fax: 44 (0) 20 8392 9876
E-mail: info@bushwoodbooks.co.uk
Website: www.bushwoodbooks.co.uk

Designed by "Sue"
Type set in Zapf Chancery Bd BT/New Baskerville BT

ISBN: 978-0-7643-4417-6
Printed in China

To P. Yogananda, Peter, Nicole,
Kristina, and Eric.

ACKNOWLEDGMENTS

I could not have written this book without the unending support of my husband, Peter, who took on the role of chauffeur, assistant, and coach throughout the entire process.

I want to gratefully acknowledge my editors, Tina Skinner and Dinah Roseberry, for their patience and strength in helping me move the project forward among many unexpected challenges and delays.

Many, many thanks to Sue Terry who volunteered her editorial talents and steadily steered me on the right linguistic path. Heartfelt thanks also to Eliana Ferrario and Natalie Seaman for their valuable input.

My deep appreciation goes to the talented photographers from all over the world who generously shared their photos of wood-fired oven and food; and to the kind people who welcomed me to their homes so that I could take pictures of their beautiful ovens and outdoor kitchens.

I am forever indebted to Nonna Isabella, Adriana, and Sira who awakened in me the passion for cooking, and who taught me so much about food.

Thank you Phil Gray for helping me with the delicate science of transferring slides to digital format.

Thank you Mom and Nicole for being such an inspiration in my life.

CONTENTS

CHAPTER ONE

ANATOMY OF A WOOD-FIRED OVEN

It was a sunny day in Naples, Italy, when I was first faced with the urgent need to learn how to cook. I was twenty years old, had just married, and was getting acquainted with my new mother-in-law. You will probably guess what her first question for me was. She inquired if I knew how to cook, and I panicked because this Italian lady came from a long line of excellent cooks and her expectations were high! I eventually recovered from the shock and ended up having a great time cooking by her side; I still cherish the traditional recipes I was taught.

Every country has its special dishes, but the Italians have developed a veritable universe of recipes and cooking techniques. Their culinary tradition goes back centuries, as does their use of wood-fired ovens. Even though the Italians didn't invent the ovens—their use started in prehistory—it was the ancient Romans who perfected the construction of ovens, using their excellent building skills and understanding of the arched dome. In the ruins of the Roman city of Pompeii[1] one can still see a large oven next to a flourmill, with an arch in brick as a cover over the opening of the oven itself and a wood storage space underneath.

The city of Naples, not far from Pompeii, is the birthplace of pizza. When the Italian queen Margherita of Savoia visited the city in 1889, she wanted to taste this local specialty and was presented a pizza topped with tomatoes, mozzarella cheese, and fresh basil, evoking the colors of the Italian flag. This selection was henceforth called the Margherita in honor of the regent and is still the most popular choice today.

It was the Italian immigrants who brought pizza to America, along with the art of building brick ovens, at the turn of the twentieth century. Although many claim to have opened the first pizzeria, most historical clues point to Gennaro Lombardi, who built a brick oven in New York around 1897, and introduced the Americans to pizza. There was no turning back after that first taste!

Two thousand year old flour mills with wood-burning oven in the background. Pompeii, Italy. *Photo by Augusto Jun Devegili.*

Detail of ancient Roman oven. Pompeii, Italy. *Photo by Augusto Jun Devegili.*

Throughout history the wood-fired oven shape has been fine-tuned, yet fundamentally, it has stayed the same: curved interior walls and dome, a flue placed at the front of the oven, which creates perfect airflow and cooking convection.

The old ovens were traditionally built out of clay, brick, or stone; they were generally large in size, with thick walls so that they would keep the retained heat needed to bake multiple batches of bread, or to roast a whole pig.

I remember when I was a child living on the island of Capri, my parents had a large brick oven and used it frequently to entertain. A *pizzaiolo*[2] would come to bake pizza, topped with the mozzarella cheese and tomatoes typical of the region, and many unforgettable summer evenings unfolded around the fire. Later on, on our farm in Tuscany, we had a beautiful communal oven that we put to work on holidays and other festivities, baking bread, traditional pastries, and once, even a whole boar.

I discovered later in life that my experience of cooking in brick ovens was a bit unusual, because World War II had destroyed the majority of the old ovens and it had become very hard to find a mason skilled in the art of repairing or making a brick oven.

After the war, when the rebuilding process was underway, the Italian government subsidized a study to find the most practical way of restoring the ovens and thus continuing the tradition of wood-fired cooking. Ingenuity arose to the occasion: the Italians merged technology and tradition by inventing the first modular wood-burning oven.

The new ovens were lighter, cost-effective, easy to transport and install on site, and took less time to heat up, a feature that proved very valuable in modern times. Italy is still the largest manufacturer of wood-burning ovens and makes some of the best on the market today.

In analyzing the differences between the old brick ovens and the new modular ovens, it is easy to see why the latter have become so popular. The masonry oven is made out of bricks and mortar, with thick walls that need to be heated for a long time before cooking. Just as it is hard to find a mason skilled in building one, it can be arduous to find the right firebrick for this building project. One must also take into consideration that regular maintenance may be needed, as in time, bricks may come lose from the dome. Nowadays, brick ovens are mostly used by bakeries or restaurants in a commercial setting, or are self-built for home use by people with a passion for these old ovens.[3]

The majority of people who are planning an outdoor entertainment center or an indoor oven for residential use will most likely choose a modular oven, because it is very easy to install, requires less maintenance, will heat up in a fraction of the time, and has proven ideal for home cooking. Modular ovens are the focus of this book and I will explain all the steps involved in building one.

Old wood-fired oven built out of rocks. These ovens are quite rare today. Filicudi, Sicily. *Photo by Roberto Zingales.*

Italian women baking traditional dishes in a modern modular oven. *Photo by Marisa Lemorande.*

WHAT IS A MODULAR OVEN?

The first feature that one will notice in looking at a modular oven is that it is made of large interconnecting pieces of refractory material. In a good oven, these pieces will connect easily and, compared to a brick oven, will actually save time and labor during the installation process.

Small modular oven with arch.

Wood-burning modular oven made of expanded clay.

A modular oven can mimic a brick oven with an added inner lining of fire-bricks.

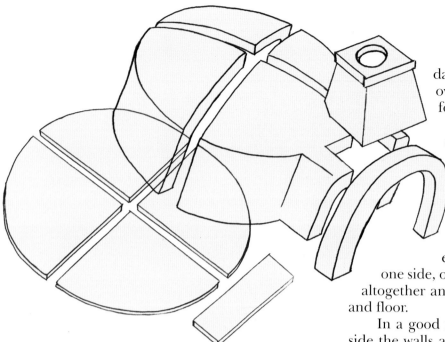

A modular oven is made of interconnecting parts.
Drawing by Gary Laib.

The refractory material has been cast and molded into the various parts of the oven, and it is able to withstand very high temperatures.

The fire is built right on the oven floor, and the smoke exits through the flue placed just above and outside the opening, leaving a surprisingly good visibility in the oven itself. The oven is shaped to allow an even airflow through the open doorway, providing fresh oxygen to the fire and heating the walls and the dome, finally flowing out of the oven through the flue. In this way, a wonderful radiating heat is created and it spells perfection for the home chef!

The right thermal mass of an oven is important, because the heat generated by the fire will absorb into the walls and floor of the oven to be later released evenly during the cooking cycle. More thermal mass means more retained heat to be released slowly after the fire is removed or dies down. The old brick ovens with their thick walls had a very large thermal mass, which also meant that it would take more than half a day to heat them up. This made sense seventy years ago in rural Italy when it was the practice of families to use the communal oven to bake their weekly batch of bread. The retained heat had to be strong enough to accommo-

date the needs of many, while today, these ovens find a better use in restaurants or for commercial purposes.

If you need an oven that heats up quickly, keeps its temperature for hours, and is versatile enough to provide for every day cooking as well as for festive occasions, then a modular oven is for you.

Once the oven has reached the desired temperature, you can cook either by moving the fire and embers to one side, or by taking out the fire and the embers altogether and using the retained heat in the walls and floor.

In a good modular oven, the floor pieces fit inside the walls and dome, separated by a small space all around, designed to allow for the floor's expansion and contraction.

When choosing a modular oven, keep in mind that the best contain a good amount of expanded clay, thus keeping the heat "trapped" for a longer time, and overall consuming less energy. Expanded clay is raw clay that has been heated in a rotating furnace to temperatures that exceed 2,200 degrees F (Fahrenheit). Before the clay reaches a liquid state, it takes the shape of small balls, which are cooled by currents of air. The result is small irregularly-formed balls similar to pumice. They have a hard crust, a porous center, and exceptional thermal properties. This process allows the inner core of the clay to capture and retain heat while the outer layer resists compression.

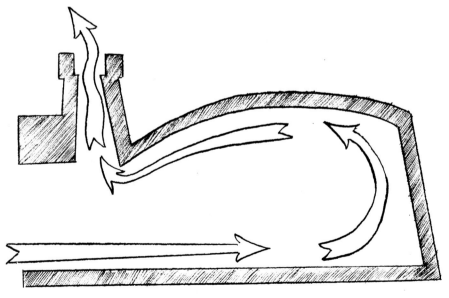

Airflow in a wood-burning oven.
Drawing by Gary Laib.

Expanded clay forms into small balls with a hard crust and a porous center.

Before outlining the steps in planning and building your oven, I want familiarize you with its components. A modular oven is made of several large pieces that are connected together at the time of installation: the floor elements, the dome pieces, the chimney manifold, and the arch.

THE FLOOR

The floor pieces are smooth, porous enough to absorb the steam generated from pizza dough (this produces that wonderful crust), yet not porous enough to absorb the spills and splatters of oil and food, which are easily burnt off in the cooking process. You could say that these ovens have a self-cleaning quality.

Floor pieces.

THE DOME

The dome of a good oven is slightly curved at the ideal height ratio, so that the air will circulate without obstruction, resulting in a perfect convection cooking. The geometry of airflow is unforgiving and if you were to build an oven that is too flat or too high, the heat would either leave out the door or a cold spot would form in the top area of the dome.

Two people can easily handle the oven dome pieces. Smaller oven models have two dome pieces that come together; larger models have four or more dome pieces.

Dome pieces interlock to form the top of the oven.

THE CHIMNEY MANIFOLD

The chimney manifold piece is placed just above and outside the oven opening. It is to this piece that the anchor plate, the chimney pipe, and chimney cap are attached (these are usually not part of a wood-fired oven kit). The best chimney manifolds are made of the same refractory material as the oven itself. Metal manifolds tend to wear out in the heat and it becomes expensive to replace them, while a refractory manifold should last as long as the oven itself.

Chimney flue.

THE ARCH

An arch is placed in front of the vent landing, that is, the main oven opening. This can be a pre-cast arch in refractory materials purchased with your oven or it can be custom made in brick, stone, or metal. An arch can also be faced with tile or stucco to conform to the overall design of your project.

Brick is a great material to showcase an oven in grand style. This pre-cast arch is faced with intricate brickwork and a beautiful keystone. *Courtesy of Michael and Karen Chidiac.*

Granite gives this pre-cast arch a wonderfully sleek and modern look. *Courtesy of Charles Flewellen.*

An oven faced with stone evokes memories of Tuscan villas. *Courtesy of Spencer Residence.*

THE DOOR

The door is usually freestanding and made of metal, wood, or refractory material. Sometimes the door is hinged to the opening, however, keep in mind this is not as practical because it takes up precious space on the landing.

When you are heating up the oven or cooking in it, you can use the door to regulate the temperature by covering the opening or placing the door on the ledge, leaning on the arch, to allow a little bit of air into the oven, or by taking the door off altogether. I will go into more detail later on how to regulate the temperature in this way.

We've looked at the different parts of a modular oven. They comprise the core of the oven itself and are part of the oven kits available on the market. In the next chapter we will explore what goes into the planning for an oven.

A metal door like this is used to seal the oven chamber.

CHAPTER TWO

PLANNING FOR YOUR OVEN

Wood-fired cooking and candle light take center stage. *Photo by Phil Gray.*

AN ITALIAN BACKYARD

Begin to plan your cooking and entertainment area by visualizing it. Imagine where you would put the oven and what would make the area surrounding it warm and inviting. Study the area from all angles and consider the overall project—not just the oven—making notes about the images you conjure and listing your needs, as well as how you want to use the area.

Will you be regularly entertaining a lot of people or just your family and a few friends? How far will the oven be located from your existing kitchen? Do you need shelter from the weather? How will the space work with other outdoor features, such as pools, playgrounds, gardens, and trees? Do you need to take into consideration special needs? This process will be the foundation of your research and planning.

Sketching is another step in the planning stage. If you plan to hire an architect or contractor, your sketches will help them understand what you have in mind.

Be sure to check with your local building inspector before starting your project. Building codes and rules for wood-fired ovens are usually covered under those for fireplaces, but they do vary and you need to follow the regulations enforced in your particular area.

DESIGNED FOR COMFORT

Outdoor cooking areas are kitchens too, so many of the same considerations apply, such as enough counter space around the wood-fired oven for food preparation. Space under the counters for storage makes it less necessary to make trips back and forth from the house. There are many varieties of outdoor shelving and cabinet doors, from stainless steel to powder-coated. You can also build your own from wood that you like.

Eating outdoors–*al fresco*–in Tuscany.

If you can't afford it or the area you will use restricts you from having enough counter space or preparation area, consider establishing your cooking area as close to your indoor kitchen as possible.

If there are limitations, begin with an oven and some counter space. You can always add other features later, as money and space permits, such as a sink, a small fridge, or other amenities. Whether your plan is limited or not, success depends on ensuring that your family and friends will be comfortable sharing meals and relaxing together around the oven.

Fireplace and oven complement each other in this intimate outdoor setting.

Comfortably shaded, this outdoor dining area is close to the wood-fired oven and will allow guests to enjoy eating *al fresco* all year round. *Courtesy of Spencer Residence.*

A high counter around an outdoor kitchen is a comfortable place to watch the chef prepare the food and keep him or her company.

Allow space for people to watch the chef, enjoy the hypnotic quality of the fire, and for traffic around the food preparation area. A raised bar around the cooking counter insures the chef will have plenty of company. If you're making pizza, you will be using long-handled tools so you need extra space in front of the oven door.

By adding one or more tables, you can create a place for people who just want to relax and not be involved in cooking or preparation.

An outside kitchen needs protection from the elements: sun or wind can be uncomfortable for your guests, so plan accordingly. A trellis with climbing plants and mature trees create shade and comfort and a healthier environment. Strategically located shrubs and fences are very effective windbreakers. I planted my herb and vegetable garden not far from my oven, so that when I need oregano, basil, arugula, or tomatoes, they are nearby.

Ample counter space with stainless steel appliances and storage doors. *Courtesy of Anthony Walton.*

For the surface of your wood-fired oven there are varieties of stones: cultured stones, stone tiles, granite, marble, ceramic tiles, brick, decorative concrete, and stucco. Choose materials that harmonize with each other and with the overall look of your home and garden. I suggest obtaining samples so you can see how they look in the area.

CHOOSING YOUR OVEN

There are several sizes of wood-burning ovens. Before you go shopping, think of how many people you usually entertain, what you will be cooking, and how much space is available for the oven. Installation costs increase minimally between the oven models so—unless the space for the oven is very small—buy a medium oven instead of a small one.

It is important to know the interior diameter of the oven so you can determine its cooking space. Keep in mind that the fire takes up a portion of that space. The interior of a small oven ranges in diameter from 30" to 35". A medium oven, from 39" to 45" and a large oven from 47" to 50" or more. Also important are the outside dimensions to make sure the oven will fit within the building plan.

OVEN CAPACITY[1]

	Pizza	Bread	Pans	Meat
	3	6	2	16 lbs. turkey
	6	12	4	Full-sized turkey
	8	14	6	Whole piglet or lamb

Once you purchased your oven, you will need to "house" it, in other words, to build a structure around it to keep it weatherproof. This is important because when heated, moisture that seeped into the oven will turn to steam that will cause cracks. The structure can be simple or elaborate depending on your budget and plan; I have included line drawings to give you a few alternatives. You can easily adapt them to your needs.

Outdoor entertainment area shaded by wood trellis.

CONCRETE MASONRY CONSTRUCTION

This is a standard concrete block and rebar structure resting on a concrete slab with footing. The base is usually set at a height between 39" and 45"; this allows the cook to use the oven without bending. The oven modules are installed on the base, and insulation and a chimney system are added. Finally, the walls are built up around it and the roof is finished.

Dining area shaded by wood trellis and bamboo. *Courtesy of Bonnie Nitta and Jack Scherrer.*

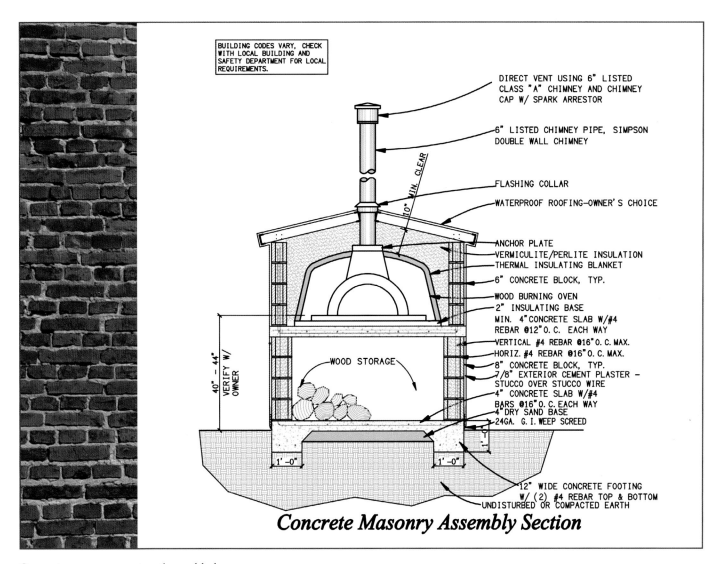

BUILDING CODES VARY, CHECK WITH LOCAL BUILDING AND SAFETY DEPARTMENT FOR LOCAL REQUIREMENTS.

DIRECT VENT USING 6" LISTED CLASS "A" CHIMNEY AND CHIMNEY CAP W/ SPARK ARRESTOR

6" LISTED CHIMNEY PIPE, SIMPSON DOUBLE WALL CHIMNEY

FLASHING COLLAR

WATERPROOF ROOFING-OWNER'S CHOICE

ANCHOR PLATE
VERMICULITE/PERLITE INSULATION
THERMAL INSULATING BLANKET
6" CONCRETE BLOCK, TYP.
WOOD BURNING OVEN
2" INSULATING BASE
MIN. 4" CONCRETE SLAB W/#4 REBAR @12" O.C. EACH WAY
VERTICAL #4 REBAR @16" O.C. MAX.
HORIZ. #4 REBAR @16" O.C. MAX.
8" CONCRETE BLOCK, TYP.
7/8" EXTERIOR CEMENT PLASTER - STUCCO OVER STUCCO WIRE
4" CONCRETE SLAB W/#4 BARS @16" O.C. EACH WAY
4" DRY SAND BASE
24GA. G.I. WEEP SCREED

10" MIN. CLEAR

40" - 44" VERIFY W/ OWNER

WOOD STORAGE

1'-0"

1'-0"

12" WIDE CONCRETE FOOTING W/ (2) #4 REBAR TOP & BOTTOM
UNDISTURBED OR COMPACTED EARTH

Concrete Masonry Assembly Section

Concrete masonry construction gable house.

CONCRETE MASONRY AND METAL FRAME CONSTRUCTION

This drawing illustrates the option of building the base in concrete block and upper portion in metal frame. You can also build the whole structure of heavy gauge metal framing anchored to a foundation. Building a metal frame is advantageous because it is lighter.

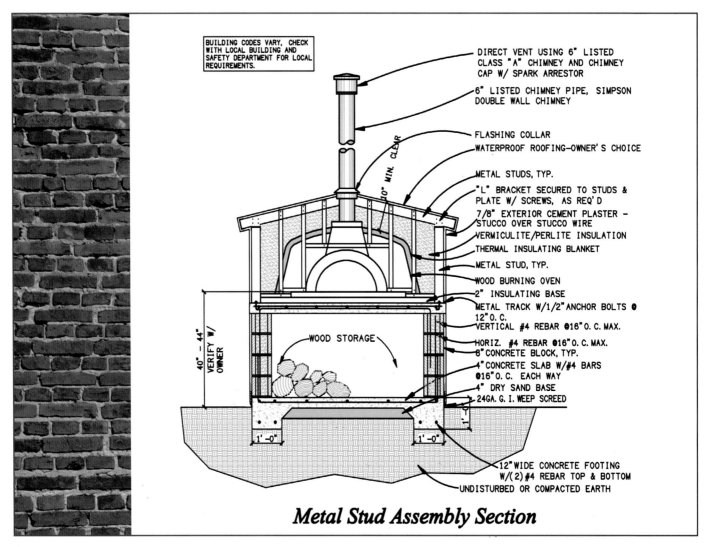

BUILDING CODES VARY, CHECK WITH LOCAL BUILDING AND SAFETY DEPARTMENT FOR LOCAL REQUIREMENTS.

DIRECT VENT USING 6" LISTED CLASS "A" CHIMNEY AND CHIMNEY CAP W/ SPARK ARRESTOR

6" LISTED CHIMNEY PIPE, SIMPSON DOUBLE WALL CHIMNEY

10" MIN. CLEAR

FLASHING COLLAR
WATERPROOF ROOFING—OWNER'S CHOICE

METAL STUDS, TYP.

"L" BRACKET SECURED TO STUDS & PLATE W/ SCREWS, AS REQ'D

7/8" EXTERIOR CEMENT PLASTER – STUCCO OVER STUCCO WIRE
VERMICULITE/PERLITE INSULATION
THERMAL INSULATING BLANKET
METAL STUD, TYP.
WOOD BURNING OVEN
2" INSULATING BASE
METAL TRACK W/1/2" ANCHOR BOLTS @ 12" O. C.
VERTICAL #4 REBAR @16" O. C. MAX.
HORIZ. #4 REBAR @16" O. C. MAX.
6" CONCRETE BLOCK, TYP.
4" CONCRETE SLAB W/#4 BARS @16" O. C. EACH WAY
4" DRY SAND BASE
24GA. G. I. WEEP SCREED

40" – 44" VERIFY W/ OWNER

WOOD STORAGE

1'-0"   1'-0"

12" WIDE CONCRETE FOOTING W/(2) #4 REBAR TOP & BOTTOM
UNDISTURBED OR COMPACTED EARTH

Metal Stud Assembly Section

Concrete masonry and metal construction gable house.

MEDITERRANEAN STYLE

The Mediterranean style is minimalist and after having constructed the base or hearth out of concrete block and rebar, the oven is covered using pencil bar and stucco mesh to follow the curvature of the dome, resulting in a rounded structure.

Now you have a general idea of the building plan and you are ready to read in more detail about the construction of the foundation and structure around the oven as well as about the installation of the oven modules. Or…you can skip ahead to the cooking section for inspiration and mouth-watering recipes!

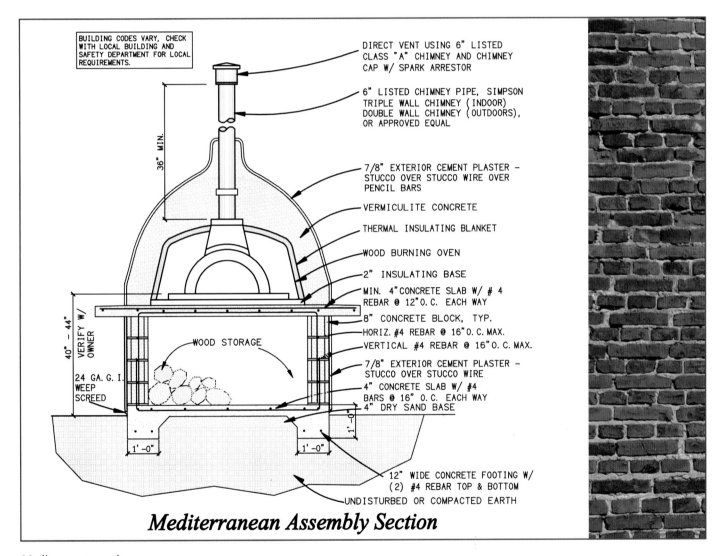

Mediterranean Assembly Section

Mediterranean style.

CHAPTER THREE

INSULATION AND VENTING MATERIALS

An oven that is properly insulated will use less wood, heat up faster and stay hot longer. Good insulation saves energy! This chapter will list the most common insulating materials used today, available from wood-fired oven companies or building material stores.

We owe a great debt to the Old World for keeping the oven tradition alive, but we have technology to thank for creative innovations when it comes to insulating materials. After a great meal at a restaurant in Sardinia[1], my husband and I inquired about their wood-fired oven, in particular what they had used for insulating it. The owner explained he had used broken bottles and filled the cavity between the concrete wall and the oven with this crushed glass. In the past, when little was available, people used what they had laying around: left-over pieces of firebrick, sand, glass, even salt. These materials are not the best solution, especially when applied to modular ovens, because they can prove too heavy and do not provide optimum insulation.

Modern insulators are less cumbersome and quickly put in place, making this step fast and economical. An insulating pad is created to set the oven on, and after the oven pieces have been assembled, more insulating material is placed on top of the oven. In the next chapter, I will go into more detail on exactly how to insulate your oven.

INSULATING PAD

Super Isol Board

This is a calcium silicate board that holds high heat and greatly reduces thermal conductivity. It also rates high in compression strength, so it can take both the heat and the weight of the oven. Another nice feature is that it is light and can easily be cut to size with regular wood working tools.

The standard size of a board is 24" x 36" and between 1 1/2" to 2" in thickness; you will need approximately 2 boards for a small oven and 3 to 4 boards for a medium-sized one.

Vermiculite and Cement Mix

Vermiculite is considered a limited-expansion clay, and comes in granules. Perlite, which has a similar use, is an amorphous volcanic glass formed into lightweight granules. Both are great insulators, but vermiculite has a higher compression strength and can be mixed with cement to create an insulating pad on top of which the oven pieces are set. (The next chapter covers the details of creating a vermiculite and cement mix.) Perlite on the other hand is better used loose as an extra insulation to fill the cavity between the wall and the oven because it can be easily crushed when mixed with heavier compounds such as cement.

Perlite is not expensive and it is sold in bags at masonry outlets. Vermiculite is harder to find, but because it is used in horticulture as well, it is usually available at garden supplies centers.

Firebrick

Bricks made of highly insulating refractory material typically used to build a brick oven, can also be used to create an insulating pad for the oven, although this is a more costly alternative, in terms of both material and labor. Use the standard, low-duty fireclay firebrick and make sure that you set them plumbed and level.

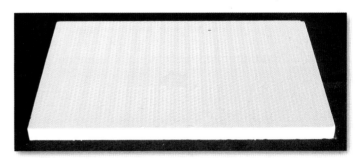
Super Isol Board.

Thermal Insulating Blanket

A calcium-magnesium-silicate fiber blanket is used for providing insulation for the top of the oven. It is very lightweight and flexible, easy to drape over the dome and helps keep the oven hot for a long time.

Vermiculite Mix

Vermiculite mixed with cement is also used to coat the dome of the oven for insulation and extra thermal mass. It can be used alone or in conjunction with a thermal insulating blanket. If used together with a thermal blanket, then the blanket is placed on top of the vermiculite mix, after it has dried.

Another alternative is to drape the blanket around the oven dome and then pour perlite or vermiculite in the loose, unmixed form to fill the cavity between the oven and the structure wall, for extra insulation.

Refractory Mortar

There are many kinds of refractory mortars on the market made of fireclay and fine sand. You will most likely be able to purchase refractory mortar with your oven. This mortar is used to set the floor pieces, to grout, and seal the joints of the dome pieces. Some refractory mortar is water-soluble, so it is best to cover any unfinished work with plastic to protect it from rain.

Chimney Pipe System

An anchor plate is placed on top of the oven's chimney flue. The chimney pipe fits onto the anchor plate, and a chimney cap with a spark arrestor is placed at the end of the pipe to prevent rain or moisture from seeping into the oven. For best draw, use a double-walled stainless-steel chimney pipe system.

Thermal insulating blanket.

CHAPTER FOUR

BUILDING THE OVEN

Building a modular wood-fired oven is generally divided into two parts:

A the creation of a structure to support and house the oven; and

B the installation of the oven modules.

Installing the modules of a wood-fired oven is straightforward and simple, but building the structure around the oven itself requires a good knowledge of how to work with mortar and block. If you don't know how to build a safe and sound structure, hire a contractor. Be sure to check your state and local codes before starting any project and follow all safety precautions.

It is a lot of fun to plan the style and the "look" of this structure, but keep in mind that the housing should be weatherproof, made of fire resistant materials, and strong enough to carry the weight of an oven.

Most people opt for a concrete block structure, but ovens can also be accommodated in heavy gauge steel and concrete backer board construction, a good solution especially for decks or patios where weight considerations are important. An alternative is a "hybrid" with the base in concrete block and the top in steel and backer board.

Whenever space, view, or design requirements dictate a smaller oven, reduce the top by following the shape of the dome using a stucco lathe.

CONCRETE SLAB FOUNDATION

Stand-alone or incorporated into an outdoor kitchen with counters and appliances, your structure requires a foundation or a reinforced concrete slab upon which to rest.

Mark the area to be excavated. When you measure the perimeter of the slab, allow extra space for the finish material. Check your local building codes to see how thick your concrete slab will have to be, and excavate the foundation to the proper depth.

Pouring the concrete slab foundation.
Drawing by Gary Laib.

Build a form with 2 x 6s. Make sure everything is square and level and that the frame is held in place securely by stakes placed at intervals of a few feet. Fill it with gravel or crushed stone, tamping it down firmly.

Run any utility lines or pipes. Install reinforcing rebar by making a grid every 2 feet, or use wire-mesh reinforcement.

Pour the concrete, filling the form to the top and then level the fresh concrete by pulling a 2 x 4 or other straight-edge tool along the top of the form until the concrete is level. Allow plenty of time for the concrete to cure and harden.

BUILDING THE BASE

The oven needs a base, about 39" to 45" high, so that you can comfortably cook without bending. The traditional design for a wood-fired oven allows for an opening in the front of the base to use as wood storage, which is practical and esthetically pleasing.

To calculate how big your base needs to be, take the outer dimensions of the oven and add a minimum of 3" on each side for clearance between the oven and the start of the wall (this includes 2" of insulation material). It is good to have a small ledge of at least 7" in front of the oven for a utensil or tool and to be able to position the door when regulating the temperature.

Concrete blocks are a popular choice for building the base because they are fire resistant, durable, and effective at reducing thermal swings. The holes inside the blocks allow the rebar and concrete to run vertically through the block, and the rebar can be anchored to the concrete slab.

Metal framing, or steel framing, is a good choice. It is fire resistant and lightweight. Concrete backer board is cut and attached to the frame, and then finished with a stone, tile, or stucco exterior.

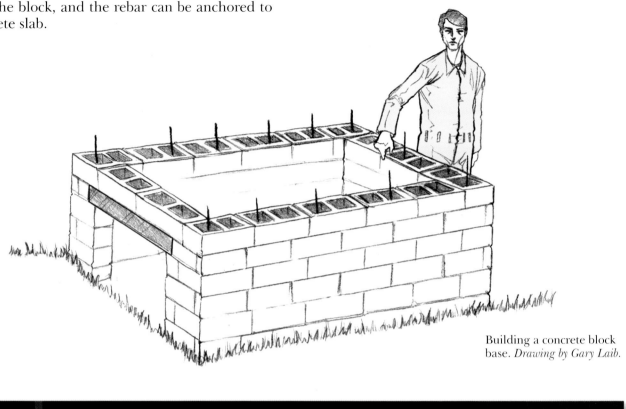

Building a concrete block base. *Drawing by Gary Laib.*

Finished base for oven and counters. *Courtesy of Design Detail.*

Concrete block base in the process of being built. *Courtesy of Anthony Carreon.*

Concrete block base with exterior finished in stone. *Courtesy of Will Eklund, Eklund Construction.*

POURING THE HEARTH SLAB

Build a frame for the bottom of the form that can be easily removed after you have poured and cured the concrete. Lay a grid of rebar and pour a layer of structural concrete.

Steel framing will later be covered with concrete backer board.

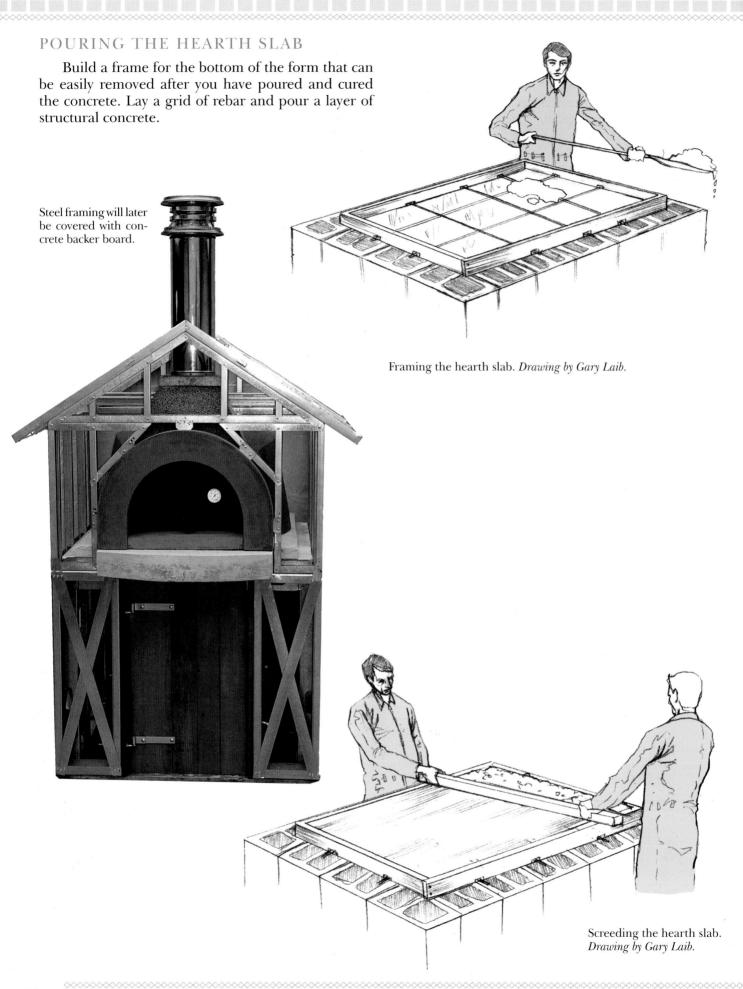

Framing the hearth slab. *Drawing by Gary Laib.*

Screeding the hearth slab. *Drawing by Gary Laib.*

CREATING AN INSULATING PAD

The creation of an insulation pad between the cement base or hearth and the oven floor pieces greatly enhances your oven's energy efficiency with minimal effort and cost. There are several ways to build an insulating pad: Super Isol boards, a vermiculite and cement mixture, or a layer of firebricks. The easiest and fastest way is Super Isol boards.

Super Isol Board Insulation Pad

These lightweight boards can be bought in the convenient size of 24" x 36" x 2". If needed, they can be cut by using regular wood working tools. (Wear a mask and eye protection when drilling or cutting Super Isol boards—they contain silica.)

Base in concrete backer board.
Courtesy of Will Eklund, Eklund Construction.

Framing of hearth slab with rebar and wire mesh.

Detail.

Concrete has been poured over the rebar and wire mesh.

Finished concrete slab ready for installation of the oven modules.

Make sure the surface on which you set them is level or they may break. (You can set them on either of their sides.) If they do break, it will not alter their performance. To set them on the cement base or hearth, use the special high-temperature glue that comes with the boards. Only a small amount is necessary; the weight of the oven holds the boards in place. Not just the floor elements of the oven but the entire oven, including the arch, will sit on the Super Isol boards, so this pad will be at least 4" larger than the outer diameter of the oven.

Super Isol boards are porous and absorb moisture so they must be stored in a dry place. Avoid moisture as much as possible! If they become wet, or even damp, the steam they would create under the oven floor may cause the oven to crack. Super Isol boards must be completely encased in the structure you are building, leaving no part of the boards exposed.

Vermiculite Insulation Pad

Build a frame for a 2"-thick pad, allowing enough space for the whole oven, including the arch, to sit. Mix 1 part of vermiculite to 3 parts of cement, slowly adding enough water until it is the consistency of oatmeal. Pour the mix in the frame, level it, and let it harden for a few days.

Fire Brick Insulation Pad

This option is labor intensive: Create a pad by setting a layer of standard, low-duty fireclay firebricks. Make certain they are plumbed and level.

Super Isol boards installed on hearth slab. *Courtesy of Sal Oliva.*

MODULAR OVEN INSTALLATION

Read the installation guidelines provided with your oven, carefully. Before you start setting everything in mortar, set up a dry installation of the oven modules on the base you built. This will give you the feel of the project and time to address questions or problems.

Once you center the oven to satisfaction, make an outline of the oven with pencil, chalk, or spray paint, and carefully remove the pieces.

Mix the refractory mortar or refractory grout following the manufacturer's instructions. Set the floor pieces first, starting with the front landing piece. This will be your cooking surface so make sure all the floor pieces are level and square with the smooth side up.

Vermiculite insulating pad on hearth slab. *Courtesy of Will Eklund, Eklund Construction.*

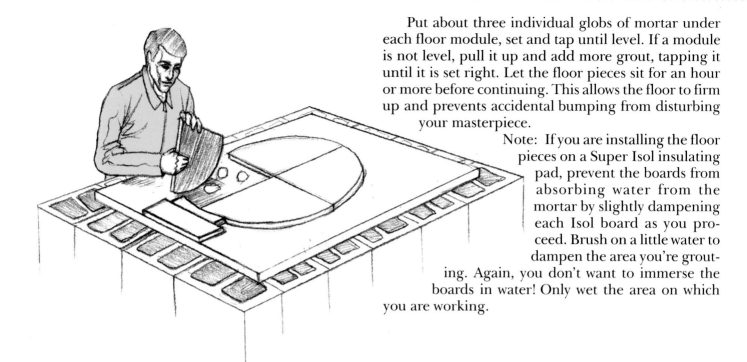

Put about three individual globs of mortar under each floor module, set and tap until level. If a module is not level, pull it up and add more grout, tapping it until it is set right. Let the floor pieces sit for an hour or more before continuing. This allows the floor to firm up and prevents accidental bumping from disturbing your masterpiece.

Note: If you are installing the floor pieces on a Super Isol insulating pad, prevent the boards from absorbing water from the mortar by slightly dampening each Isol board as you proceed. Brush on a little water to dampen the area you're grouting. Again, you don't want to immerse the boards in water! Only wet the area on which you are working.

Installing the floor modules.
Drawing by Gary Laib.

Floor modules are set with refractory grout. *Courtesy of Will Eklund, Eklund Construction.*

Next, set the dome pieces. Some ovens need a little grout between the seams, others require a dry installation. In grouting the female and male grooves of the dome pieces, remember that you need a very little amount of grout. The dome pieces are not grouted to the base, nor are the dome pieces and the floor pieces grouted together. It is important that these are left grout-less and dry to allow for the expansion and contraction of the oven as it heats and cools, or the oven will crack.

Refractory mortar.

Placing the floor modules.

Floor modules set on the cement slab.

Begin by placing the male dome module. Remember to support it or have someone hold it. Lightly grout the grooves of the female module; then join it to the other piece. If you put too much grout in the groove it will be squeezed out when you join the pieces affecting the way the oven looks—you want your oven to have a nice clean appearance.

After the dome elements are set, look inside the oven. You will notice an empty space all around where the floor meets the dome walls. This is the expansion space and should *never* be grouted.

Apply a strip of refractory grout across the outside seams of the dome to seal the dome joints. Don't grout the seams inside the oven.

A dome piece of a small oven with the line of grout placed in the seam.

Setting the other dome piece and the flue completes the oven.

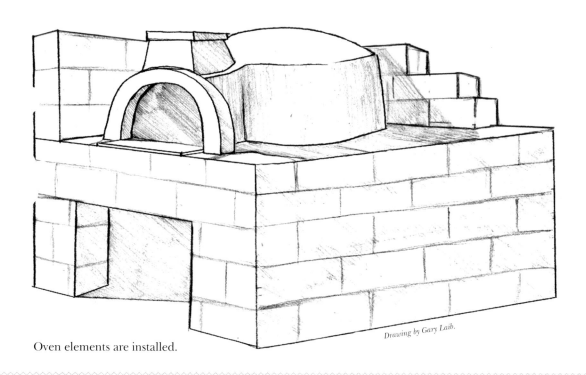

Drawing by Gary Laib.

Oven elements are installed.

SETTING THE CHIMNEY FLUE

Install the chimney flue over the opening using the refractory mortar. If your oven has two entry elements that hold up the chimney flue, you can use polymer-modified Thinset mortar (find it at your builder's supplies store). Hold elements in place while the mortar sets. Grout the seams around the front floor piece with the same Thinset (remember not to grout the seams on the inside of the oven).

Install the chimney flue over the opening using the refractory mortar. Keep the flue flush with the front edge of the dome and add mortar to the back, if needed, to make it level. The chimney flue is usually made of 2 parts: a main piece and a connector piece that fits the stainless steel anchor plate and the chimney pipe.

For outdoor use, you need a stainless steel, class A (also called UL103HT) double-walled chimney system.

Chimney flue and connector are set with mortar.
Courtesy of Will Eklund, Eklund Construction.

Attach the chimney pipe sections to reach the desired height. A minimum of 36" length of pipe is recommended for best draw and functionality. Top the pipe with a stainless steel chimney cap and spark arrestor. If you are building a chimney in masonry, top the chimney pipe to avoid allowing moisture to seep into the oven through the chimney pipe.

Oven with sealed seams and installed chimney flue. *Courtesy of Will Eklund, Eklund Construction.*

Stainless steel anchor plate, chimney pipe, and chimney cap installed. *Courtesy of Will Eklund, Eklund Construction.*

ARCH

You can build your own arch or buy a prefabricated one. Attach it to the oven either with refractory mortar, polymer-modified Thinset mortar, or high temperature caulk. Put a dab of the mortar on the bottom of the arch and generous amounts on the backside that touches the oven. Set and hold in place.

THERMAL INSULATING BLANKET

If you are insulating the dome with a thermal insulating blanket, drape it over the dome. Overlap the seams of the blanket whenever possible. Use protective long sleeves and gloves when handling the insulating blanket. Fill the cavity between the oven and the structure walls with loose vermiculite or perlite, covering the oven entirely.

VERMICULITE OR PERLITE COATING

This mixture is used to coat the dome providing extra insulation and thermal mass. Mix 6 parts of vermiculite or perlite to 1 part of cement, slowly adding enough water until the mixture has the consistency of oatmeal. Cover the dome of the oven with a 2" to 3" thick coating of this mixture.

If a stronger insulation is needed—in colder areas of the country for example, or in situations where extra insulation is an asset—a thermal insulating blanket can be draped over the coated dome.

You have completed the installation and insulation of the oven modules. All that remains is finishing the housing structure, including the roof.

The arch is set and held in place. All the oven modules have been assembled on top of an insulating layer of Super Isol Boards that have been cut to follow the outline of the oven.

The oven dome is wrapped in a thermal insulating blanket.

A coating of vermiculite and cement has been applied on top of the oven.

Stucco has been applied to seal the oven; it will then be painted with exterior stucco paint to make the surface impermeable.

CHAPTER FIVE

CURING AND THE FIRST FIRING OF YOUR OVEN

When you finish building your oven, you will have a wonderful feeling of accomplishment! There's only one more step before you triumphantly fire your oven for the first time: All residual moisture must be eliminated from the oven.

Curing is the gradual elimination of moisture that may have settled in the oven walls and floor during the building process. Up to 5 gallons of moisture could be present in a medium oven and must be slowly eliminated. If you don't dry your oven properly before the first firing, heat will turn moisture into steam expanding its volume up to 30 times. Steam exerts a strong mechanical action that may crack your oven.

The best way to dry the oven is: Wait. How long depends on the manufacturer's guidelines. If you have insulated the dome with a thermal blanket and kept the oven elements dry during construction, you can get away with about 10 days. If you coated the dome with vermiculite and cement or a similar mixture, the oven will have absorbed water. Then, it is better to wait about 20 days.

Check inside the oven. Dark areas on the walls indicate moisture is present. Remember, weather and climate effect waiting time. A dry summer in Arizona versus a wet fall in Connecticut will make a difference…

PRE-FIRING YOUR OVEN

After the waiting period, pre-fire your oven. Slowly, and with relatively low temperature, this process dries residual moisture in the oven and in the mortar surrounding it. Before starting your first "real" fire, it is very important to create heat that is "even" —without spikes or high flames. Check the manufacturer's instructions and always follow them—better to be safe than sorry.

Never fire up an oven that has not been fully insulated and encased.

A simple way to pre-fire is to use plain barbeque charcoal—without starter fluid. This is for safety reasons and also because the fluid would leave a bad taste in your food! Because the oven is a closed environment, you should never use liquid starter fuels such as gasoline, gasoline-type fuel, lantern fuel, kerosene, charcoal lighter fuel, or similar liquids!

Use a chimney starter or your barbecue grill to start the charcoals then transfer them into the oven. Distribute them evenly in a single layer covering the whole oven floor. Leave the oven door off during this process so the oven will dry. Let the charcoal fire die and the oven cool for 24 hours. Repeat this procedure once a day for three consecutive days using about one bag of plain barbecue charcoal for each pre-firing.

Do not build a large, hot fire right away. It may cause the oven to crack. Hairline cracks are not a problem; they are normal. I am referring to large cracks.

During its long life span, if you notice that your wood-fired oven has absorbed moisture, repeat the pre-firing process and cure it again before you fire it up for the season.

ABOUT WOOD

The kind of wood is very important for the proper functioning of the oven. I can't emphasize this enough: seasoned, dry hardwood is essential! Wet or resinous wood will smolder and produce black smoke that will not heat your oven and could eventually ruin the oven floor.

Firewood is generally divided between two broad categories: hardwood and softwood. Hardwoods come from deciduous, broad-leafed trees; softwoods come from needle-bearing coniferous trees. Hardwood is denser and less resinous, producing a fire that is hotter and cleaner than softwood.

Ash, almond, avocado, beech, birch, oak, fruitwood (cherry, peach, plum are great), walnut, hickory, olive, maple, pecan, and mesquite are all excellent hardwoods for your oven. Eucalyptus is okay, though a bit oily. Avoid using resinous wood such as pine or spruce, and definitely do not use treated wood such as lumber.

Burning hardwood emits a wonderful fragrance while enhancing the taste of your dishes. The wood must be dry. Fresh cut wood or green wood has too much moisture and should not be used. Moisture content of the wood must be no more than 20 percent—this usually takes 6 months of reasonable weather. Seasoning is complete in one year; in two years, the wood is as dry as it can be.

Seasoned wood has cracking on the ends of the logs and is dull in color. Smack two pieces together: A "thud" sound indicates the wood is green; a "thunk" indicates dry wood. Firewood is sold by the cord, which equals 128 cubic feet and measures 4 x 4 x 8 feet. Hardwood is occasionally available at no cost from local parks, recreation facilities, farms, and gardeners after a pruning job.

Wood dries faster if it is split and stacked properly. Choose a protected and ventilated sunny spot with a supporting base that is off the ground. Crisscross layers of logs alternating the direction of each layer. During rainy or snowy weather, cover the woodpile with a tarp placing a few rocks or bricks between the wood and the tarp. This keeps the tarp elevated and prevents moisture from getting trapped between the wood and the tarp.

A good stack of dry hardwood is needed.

STARTING THE FIRE

Place a cube of non-toxic firestarter (such as Weber) or crumpled newspaper in the center of your oven floor. On top of this, add small pieces of dry, split hardwood and two or three larger pieces. Light the firestarter. The flame will reach the top of the dome and leap forward toward the chimney.

If smoke comes out of the opening, place the door on the landing, leaving a small gap. This will coax the smoke to exit through the chimney flue. Once the oven walls heat up, then the smoke will easily flow through the flue and you can take the door off.

After 15 minutes or so, move the fire towards the back of the oven. Gradually add wood as needed to keep the fire going. Soot from the fire will make the top of the oven black. After one hour or more, the soot disappears, leaving the dome white and looking like new. This means the oven is hot enough for cooking. Take your first temperature read. The oven should be about 850+ degrees F.

Most of the fire is now reduced to embers. To prepare for cooking, move the fire or embers to the left or the right of the oven. Leave the door open so the oven can cool to about 750-650 degrees F, which is perfect for your pizza.

Unless it is an emergency, never use water to lower temperature of the oven or to extinguish the fire. If you need to diminish or snuff out the fire, close the door. Without a fresh supply of oxygen, the fire will die. It is not a good idea to "mop" the floor or introduce too much water into an oven. If you are in doubt about how to keep your oven clean, ask the manufacturer. Keep moisture out of the refractory clay elements to avoid cracks.

The first firing of an oven is an exciting time, and for many, the beginning of a passion. There is absolutely no substitute for the taste of food cooked with fire! Preparing food in this type of oven and serving it under a blue evening sky is a deeply satisfying experience for you and for your guests. Personally, I love to prepare meals this way, and I welcome this break in my busy life. It's a great way to spend time with my family and friends… and it's right in my own backyard!

Non-toxic firestarter.

Stack small pieces of wood with larger ones.

Place firestarter under the wood stack, and soon, flames leap to the top of the dome.

Fire has been moved towards the back.

Place the door on the landing to avoid smoke.

CHAPTER SIX

TOOLS AND ACCESSORIES

It is helpful to have the right tools in order to safely manage the fire and cook comfortably. Here is a list of my favorite oven essentials. For me, they make preparing meals in a wood-fired oven easier—they will do the same for you. You will be able to find them in a hardware store, a cooking store, online, or from a company that sells wood-fired ovens.

FIRESTARTERS

What works best to start the fire is a square of non-toxic fire starter, because it does the job quickly and makes the least amount of smoke. Or you can use newspaper and kindling wood. However, nothing will work on wood that is not dry. Wet wood will just make a lot of smoke and no heat, so be sure to use dry hardwood.

GLOVES

Protect your hands! Be sure you buy gloves that withstand temperatures of 500 degrees F or higher.

ASH STICK

When the oven is ready to start cooking, use a heavy-duty flat aluminum or stainless steel stick and move the fire and the embers to the right or the left side of the oven near the wall.

Ash stick.

FLOOR BRUSH

Wait about 10 minutes to allow the temperature to equalize and the embers to die; then use a floor brush to remove smaller debris and ashes. Use a natural fiber brush rather than one with brass or metal. A wayward metal bristle could end up in your food. A natural bristle will simply burn so do not let the brush touch the fire! Brush the floor you cleared with quick movements and clean the light ash dust.

WOOD PEEL

This is a tool you may have seen in action in a restaurant or perhaps used at home. The wood peel slides pizza and bread into the oven. Pizza pies are placed directly on a lightly-floured wood peel, dressed with toppings, then placed on the hot oven floor. To slide pizza or bread onto the oven floor, gently shake the wood peel forward and backward.

There are short-handled and long-handled peels. Use one that has a long handle, unless you don't have a lot of space in front of the oven. Also, the peel surface should be big enough so uncooked pizza doesn't droop over its sides.

PIZZA TURNER

When the pizza is halfway through its cooking cycle, with a slight upward and counterclockwise motion, use a metal peel to rotate it so the other side faces the fire. Use it also to pull the pizza out of the oven when it is done.

Metal peels are best because it is difficult to get pizza or bread out of the oven with a wood peel or with a rectangular metal peel. The thin, smooth surface of a stainless steel or aluminum peel makes it easy to slide under a pizza, cooked or uncooked.

Natural fiber floor brush.

Opposite, top:
Wood peel.

Opposite, bottom:
Pizza turner.

Bubble popper.

BUBBLE POPPER

This tool is used to pop bubbles that appear on a cooking pizza. I also use it to grab hot pans by their handles and slide them out of the oven, or to move them around inside the oven.

GRILL

Most people associate grilling with a barbecue. What you may not know is that thanks to immediate searing from all sides, grilling in a wood-fired oven makes everything juicier. This is due to the fact that heat radiates from the dome and the floor and not just from the fire.

When I have a great wood fire burning in my oven, I often place a grill right on the embers and use it for fish, meat, vegetables, mushrooms, lobster, or shrimp. If you want to do this, use a heavy-gauge stainless-steel or cast-aluminum grill with sturdy legs and make certain you check the width, it has to fit through the oven door.

ASH BIN

You may eventually want to bake bread or cook certain foods with the retained heat in the oven. If so, you must have a strong fireproof metal bin with a lid to scoop up the coals and store the scooped up coals.

THERMOMETER

An infrared laser thermometer that goes up to 1,000 degrees is best for a foolproof read of oven temperature. Aim the laser pointer anywhere inside the oven and the temperature pops up on the digital display.

To calculate the oven temperature when you are cooking or following a recipe, point the laser beam to the floor of the oven and take a read of that temperature.

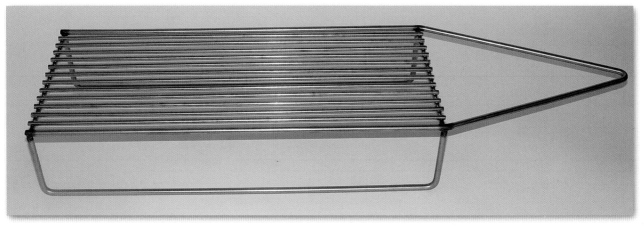

Freestanding grill.

Also keep a small, free-standing stainless steel thermometer handy for cooking in temperatures between 550 and 150 degrees F. Set it on the oven floor so you can tell how hot the oven is with the door closed. When you bake bread or a pot of beans, for example, it is important to know how much variation of heat there will be when you close the door.

Pointing a laser thermometer from a safe distance is the most accurate way to read the temperature in a hot oven.

A round metal pizza turner is the best tool to slide your pizza or bread out of the oven.

You can use a variety of pans in the oven.

COOKWARE

Metal pans with metal handles work best in high temperatures. Cast-iron pots and pans are especially suitable. You can use your regular oven cookware provided you check the manufacturer's instructions. For example, never place Pyrex glass next to the fire and use only in low temperatures. Most terracotta bake ware is for use at lower temperatures only, however, there is terracotta bake ware resistant to 1,500 degrees F.

STORAGE AND RACKS

Items such as the ashbin may be stored along with the wood under the oven. A free standing rack or a rack that hangs on the side of the oven may be used for stainless steel or aluminum tools. A shelf that slides out of the upper part of the wood storage under the oven can be installed and used to store tools, especially your wood peels—they must have shelter from moisture.

Your metal tools may be washed and scrubbed with detergent. Clean your grill with a metal brush or place it on the hot coals for 5 minutes prior to cooking.

The wood peels are wiped with a clean, moist rag. Lightly sand them whenever needed.

A NOTE ABOUT SAFETY

You are playing with fire! Be careful and be cautious—it is very hot inside your oven. Hot metal tools and pans can burn your hands—always wear gloves! If you rake the embers from the oven, wait until they are totally cold, then submerge them in water before using them in your compost or putting them in the garbage. The only fire you want to start is inside that beautiful oven of yours!

CHAPTER SEVEN

COOKING IN A WOOD-FIRED OVEN

Once you know how to check and adjust the temperature, you will discover that cooking in your wood-fired oven isn't much different from cooking in your regular oven. And you will love its wonderful, even, radiating heat. There's a learning curve, but it is a pretty simple one.

To maintain temperature, your gas or electrical oven must turn itself on and off, creating high and low spikes in the cooking process. Wood-fired ovens, however, radiate even heat throughout the cooking cycle. (Once the wood-fired oven is hot, it retains heat for many hours, and will most likely still be at about 150 degrees F the next day.) A wood-fired oven will easily register 800+ degrees F on the dome and 700+ degrees F on the floor. This cooks a pizza to perfection in just 2-3 minutes.

A refractory clay oven always retains a certain amount of moisture so you don't have to worry about food drying out. This is an important aspect when you bake pizza and bread and is definitely a great advantage when you cook a turkey or a roast.

To function at full capacity, the oven must have enough retained heat in its walls and floor, so build a good-sized fire with dry hardwood and the oven will do its job. The time it takes to pre-heat the oven varies, depending on what you're planning to cook and for how long. If you and your family yearn for a few quick pizzas on a weeknight or perhaps fish or meat on the grill, you can get away with less pre-heating time. If you are going to cook a feast such as Thanksgiving dinner or bake several loaves of bread (which requires a lot of retained heat), then preheat your oven an extra hour or so.

A Sicilian pizza and calzone like this are the exclusive product of a wood-fired oven! *Courtesy of Thomas Reichart.*

CHECKING AND REGULATING THE TEMPERATURE

The most effective way of checking temperature is with a handheld laser thermometer which can be used at a safe distance for a foolproof read. In the absence of this gadget, you can use a freestanding metal thermometer that can be found at the supermarket or hardware store. Place the thermometer on the floor at a good distance from the flame and wait about a minute for the read.

Oven kits usually have a thermometer on the door or on the outside of the oven wall. These readings although helpful, are not reliable. They only tell the temperature near the door or the wall, not the floor or the middle of the oven where you will be cooking. Over time and with experience, you will be able to adequately judge how hot the oven is.

When you want the oven to cool, leave the door off. To increase heat, close the door or add a few logs to the embers. To maintain heat, position the door on the landing or just inside the arch. When needed, racking the embers from the side of the oven to the center of the floor will heat that area quickly. After your fire has burned for about 1 to 1 ½ hours, and the oven is thoroughly heated, the temperature will be over 850 degrees F. To start cooking, let the oven cool down a bit. Don't add more wood and leave the door off.

TEMPERATURE GUIDE		
	700-650 F	Pizza
	650-600 F	Grill
	550-500 F	Roast, turkey, chicken, lamb
	550-500 F	Pan dishes
	500-400 F	Bread
	400-350 F	Desserts
	350-300 F	Beans

COOKING WITH A FLAME OR WITH DIRECT HEAT

Cooking with flame is done by moving the fire to the right or left side of the oven, letting the high flame drop, and keeping a small flame going throughout the cooking process. Pizza is baked this way, directly on the hot floor. The hot air flows from the sides to the rounded dome and back to the oven floor, quickly re-heating the floor between pizzas. The advantage of direct heat cooking is that you can leave the door open to keep an eye on what you're cooking. Direct heat cooking also gives a nice smoky fragrance to all your dishes. The temperature will usually keep between 600 F and 450 F.

GRILLING

Thanks to the convection flow of heat, grilling in a wood-burning oven gives excellent results. Food becomes crisp on the outside and stays juicy inside. Move the embers to the front-middle of the oven floor and place a freestanding grill on top. Before you add your steak, fish, lobster, shrimp, mushrooms, or vegetables, add a few small pieces of wood—a fragrant variety such as mesquite—and keep the door off, because the food cooks quickly!

COOKING WITHOUT A FLAME OR WITH INDIRECT HEAT

To bake bread or wonderful pies and desserts, roast meat, fish, and many other dishes, the temperature should be about 500 degrees F, dropping very gradually. Fire the oven well, so enough indirect heat accumulates in the walls and floors, then scoop out the coals and embers. If you're going to bake beans, wait until the temperature is around 350 degrees F. To prevent the oven from cooling down too quickly, keep the door closed and open it as little as possible.

Here, the fire has been moved to the right side of the oven to heat that area quickly.

As you learn to use your wood-fired oven, you will discover a brand new culinary experience. It is very rewarding, joining with family and friends and delicious meals around the fire.

Cooking with the direct heat of the fire.
Photo by Thomas Trocino.

Bread baked in a wood-burning oven is delicious!
Photo by Brett Hayton.

THE JOY OF
wood-fired
COOKING

PIZZA

It is faster to make your own pizza dough, rather than go out and buy it. It is a simple process and you will quickly get the hang of it, especially if you use a Kitchen-Aid mixer or other food processor with a dough hook. The sticky pizza dough is handled more efficiently by a machine than by hand.

Pizza Napoletana

Sponge:
1 package (2 ½ teaspoons) active dry yeast
1 cup lukewarm water
1 teaspoon sugar
1 tablespoon flour

Dough:
1 sponge (recipe above)
4 ½ cups unbleached organic flour, sifted
1 cup lukewarm water
2 tablespoons olive oil
1 tablespoon salt

In a large bowl, combine all sponge ingredients. Whisk well. Cover with a cloth and let sit 15 minutes. Sponge mixture should look foamy. If it does not look foamy, redo by either cooling or lowering the temperature of the water. If you do this twice and yeast does not foam, you may need new yeast.

To make the dough, put 4 ½ cups of flour, water, olive oil, and salt into the bowl with the sponge mixture. Mix well in a mixer or a food processor with a dough hook for 5 to 6 minutes. Alternatively, you can mix by hand, keeping in mind that the dough will be, and should be, very sticky—so, flour your hands well before handling.

Divide the dough into 4 quarters, using a scale to make sure they are the same weight, and shape into slightly round disks for four 10-inch pizzas. For larger pizzas, divide into 3 pieces. Lightly flour four 8-inch plastic containers with lids and put one ball of dough in each. Put the lid on, and let dough rise 2 hours in a consistently warm environment.

While the pizza dough is rising, start a good fire in your oven. It will take between approximately 1 and 1½ hours to get it ready. When the oven has reached a temperature of about 650-750 degrees F, you can start baking your pizza. Simply move the embers laterally to the right or left side of the oven with an ash stick, wait 10 minutes, and then brush the floor.

Spread ½ cup of flour on a large dinner plate. Take the dough from one of the containers and place it on the plate. Press the dough very gently into the flour, flip it over and flour the other side as well. This will make it much easier to shape the sticky dough into a round pizza pie. With your fingers and the palm of your hand work the dough outward from the center, turning the pie around a few times during this process, until it has reached a thickness of about ½ inch. You can also use a rolling pin, taking care not to push down too hard. Lightly flour a wood peel with your hands, rubbing the flour in a circular motion so that it covers the whole peel.

Place the pizza pie on the floured wood peel and garnish with toppings of your choice. The trick is not to let the pizza sit on the peel for a long time because it will stick; just garnish and slide directly onto the hot oven floor. After about 1½ minutes, rotate your pizza with a metal turner so that the other side is facing the fire. In another 1½ minutes, the pizza is ready to take out of the oven.

Pizza Margherita

A few tablespoons of crushed tomato sauce directly from the can (spread with the spoon in a circular motion)
Fresh mozzarella cheese cut into cubes
Handful of fresh basil leaves
Olive oil sprinkled on top

Follow dough recipe on page 63; use above toppings before placing in the wood-fired oven.

Garnishing your pizzas is the fun part. *Photo by Brett Hayton.*

Pizza Arugola e Tartufo

Equal parts fresh mozzarella and Italian fontina cheeses, cut into cubes
One handful of fresh arugula
Truffle oil

This is a *pizza bianca*, or white pizza, with no tomato sauce. Follow the dough recipe on page 63. Garnish the pizza with the cheese. Cook in the oven and, before serving, arrange a handful of arugula leaves over the pizza, and sprinkle truffle oil on top.

Garnishing a pizza pie with black olives and mushrooms.

Pizza all'Uovo

A few tablespoons crushed tomato sauce
Fresh mozzarella cheese cut into cubes
Olive oil sprinkled on top
One egg
Ham cut into small cubes

A wood-fired oven is hot enough to cook an egg on your pizza! Follow the dough recipe on page 63. Spread the tomato sauce with a spoon over the pizza pie. Add the cheese. Break a fresh egg in the middle of the pizza (it will cook sunny side up) and add the ham cubes around it. Carefully slide the pizza pie in the oven without disturbing the egg. Bake pizza, and enjoy.

A WORD ABOUT INGREDIENTS

The better the quality, the tastier the pizza. Italian Fontina, Parmesan, and Pecorino cheeses are delicious and a great complement to fresh mozzarella. Cut the cheese in small cubes instead of shredding it, this will keep it from burning in the hot oven.

When you give a pizza party, have all of your ingredients and toppings ready! When you cook pizza, everything happens very fast. If, after you have baked a few pizzas, you find that the oven floor has cooled, make sure to keep a small flame on the embers you pushed to the side, it will ensure that the heat reaches the floor, raising its temperature.

Pizza napoletana with mushrooms and olives. Buon appetito!

Dust the peel with flour so that the pizza won't stick when you slide it in the oven. *Courtesy of Michael Manetas.*

BREAD

Making bread is my favorite use of the oven; there's something very comforting about baking and eating a homemade loaf.

The first order of business is to create a *biga* or sourdough starter. The purpose of the *biga* is to grow natural yeasts used to leaven the dough and add flavor to the bread.

Biga

¾ cup all purpose white flour
(unbleached organic flour is best)
½ cup tepid water

Mix the flour and water in a small plastic or glass bowl until it is a thick sticky paste. Cover with a damp cloth (such as cheesecloth) and secure it with an elastic band. Keep it in a draft-free area (the kitchen usually is the best place), and let is sit between 2 and 4 days or until the paste looks bubbly and has a slightly sour and milky scent. If the starter has no bubbles or has an unpleasant odor, throw it away and start over.

If the paste is bubbly, the *biga* is ready for the first "feeding". Add another ¾ cup of flour and enough tepid water to make a soft, sticky, pasty dough. Work the dough with your hands or a wooden spoon to get air into the mixture. Cover with a damp cloth as before and let sit for 24 hours.

The starter should have a bubbly surface. Stir it well and discard half of it. Add another feeding of a ¾ cup of flour and tepid water as before. Cover with a damp cloth and leave for 12 hours.

In a small glass bowl, dissolve ½ teaspoon active dry yeast in ½ cup of warm water (105 degrees F). Let it sit 15 minutes until creamy, then add it to the *biga* with ½ cup of flour. Mix well and refrigerate in a glass or plastic container with the lid on. Let it ferment for 24 hours before using.

NO-KNEAD BREAD METHOD

If your time to bake bread is limited, then this method is recommended. It is very fast and will provide you with a satisfying batch of bread. See the "Resources" section of this book for more information on the No-Knead Bread. You will also find links and comments about flour.

TIP:

Use spring water or filtered water. If you use tap water, filter it, boil it, and then cool it before using. Chlorine or other chemicals impede the formation of yeast.

Pane Casareccio

MAKES TWO LARGE LOAVES

1½ teaspoons active dry yeast
½ cup warm water (105 degrees)
7 cups unbleached bread flour
1 tablespoon salt
2 ¾ cups cool water
¾ cup *biga* (see page 67)
Extra flour for work surface
Olive oil

In a small bowl, dissolve the dry yeast in the warm water. Set aside for 15 minutes until creamy.

Place the flour in a large bowl. (Do not use metal bowls or utensils as certain metals may react adversely with yeast.) Evenly mix the salt and the flour. Make a "well" in the center of the flour and add the yeast mix, cool water, and *biga*.

Mix with a wooden spoon, then with your hands kneading the dough vigorously for about 5 minutes until the dough comes away cleanly from the sides.

Turn the dough out on a clean, lightly-floured work surface. Flour your hands well and begin using the heel of your hands to compress and push the dough away from you, then fold it back over itself. Turn the dough a little, repeating the compressing and pushing away motions. If the dough is very sticky, add a little flour slowly while kneading. Make sure you have a comfortable work place so you can put the weight of your body into the kneading. This will take about 15 to 20 minutes.

The dough should become smooth, stretchy, and slightly shiny, almost satiny. The elasticity tells you the proteins are strong and evenly distributed throughout the dough. The bread is now ready to rise. Shape the dough into a ball.

Rub a large bowl with olive oil and put the dough in the bowl turning it so the olive oil coats all sides. Cover with a towel and let the dough rise at room tempera-ture (about 70 degrees F), in a draft-free corner of the kitchen, until doubled. This takes about 1 ½ hours.

Punch the dough down, fold the edges in, and turn it so the smooth side is up. Cover with a towel and let rise again until doubled. About 1 hour.

Now, it is time to fire up your oven so that wonderful retained heat accumulates for your bread baking. Let the fire burn for about 1 ½ hours then rake the embers out of the oven. The temperature should be between 500 and 400 degrees F. Close the door until you are ready to place the dough in the oven.

When the dough has doubled, turn it onto a lightly-floured work surface. With a sharp knife, divide the dough into 2 equal portions. Lightly handle each portion, gently folding the edges toward the center, forming a round ball with a smooth side.

Dust a generous layer of flour on a cookie sheet and place the ball of dough with the rough side down on the flour.

Cover the loaves again with a towel and let them rise for about 45 minutes. When the dough has risen, take the cookie sheet with the loaves to the oven. The oven temperature should be between 500-400 degrees F. Dust the wood peel with flour by spreading it with your hand in a circular motion. Gently slide your hand under a loaf and turn it onto the peel with its rough side up. It is okay if there is a dusting of flour on top of the loaf. Slide the loaf directly onto the floor of the oven by gently shaking the peel in a forward and backward motion. Repeat the operation with the second loaf. Close the oven door tightly.

The bread will be done in about 30 minutes and will have an attractive golden-brown color with a pattern of white flour on top. Tapping the bottom of the bread should produce a hollow sound. When you insert a food thermometer into the middle of the bread, it should read 200 degrees F.

Wait one hour before cutting and eating. Although the tempting look, feel, and aroma of the bread makes waiting difficult, it will enhance the taste of the bread.

MEAT & FISH

This recipe is for those who like tender, moist breast meat, crisp skin, and overcooked thigh meat.

Roast Chicken

SERVES FOUR

One 2 ½ - 3 lbs free-range chicken
3 handfuls of fresh herbs (such as sage, parsley, and thyme) finely chopped
¼ cup olive oil
1 lemon, halved
4 bay leaves, torn
2 sprigs of fresh rosemary
2 cloves of garlic
Sea salt and freshly ground black pepper

Put the roasting tray in a 500 degree F oven. Wash the chicken inside and out, and pat dry with paper towels. Rub the cavity with salt. Very carefully, grab the skin at the tip of the chicken breasts, making sure it doesn't rip, and pull up gently. With your other hand, gently separate the skin from the meat of the breasts so you have two little tunnels on each side. Sprinkle a little salt into the gaps, push in the chopped herbs, and drizzle in a little olive oil.

Stuff the lemon, bay leaves, garlic, and rosemary into the main chicken cavity. Pull the skin of the chicken breasts forward so that none of the flesh is exposed, then tuck the little winglets under, and tie up as firmly as possible with kitchen twine.

Rub olive oil and leftover chopped herbs into the skin of the chicken and season very generously with salt and pepper.

Remove the hot roasting tray from the oven and add a little oil. Place the chicken on its side, breast side down on the tray and put it in the oven. Cook for about 5 minutes, then turn it on its other side, breast side down. Cook for another 5 minutes, then place the chicken on its back. Cook for about 1 hour. The skin should be really crispy and the herbs will have flavored the flesh.

Bistecca alla Fiorentina (TUSCAN PORTERHOUSE)

SERVES TWO TO THREE

1 (2 1/2 pound) choice or prime porterhouse steak, cut 2- to 3-inch thick
3 tablespoons olive oil
Sea salt, coarse

This famous Tuscan steak is made from the local Chianina breed of cattle, which is prized for tenderness and flavor. Do like the Italians: use top choice meat and pay attention to the quality of the wood to bring out the satisfying grilled flavor that the simplicity of this dish demands.

The meat should be at room temperature for one hour; this is very important. Take your meat out of the fridge and start the fire in your pizza oven using hickory, oak, or another hardwood that is dry and split. After about one hour, the coals should be white hot. Rake them out to a 2- to 3-inch bed that extends about 3 inches beyond the grill itself for uniform heat. The coals should be placed to the front section of the oven. Push the rest of the fire to one side. Slide a metal grill on 3-inch high stands over the coals. Let it heat up for 5 minutes then slide out and grease with a piece of fat, or a clean cloth dipped in olive oil.

Gently brush or rub olive oil onto the steak, then season to taste with sea salt. Place the meat on the grill (it should sizzle), slide it into the oven, and don't move the steak. After about 3 to 5 minutes check the sear marks and rotate the meat 90 degrees to give it a nice crosshatch pattern. After another 2 minutes, turn the steak and cook the other side for 3 to 5 minutes.

Remove, place on a platter, season to taste, and let it rest for 5 minutes before serving.

Wood–Roasted Salmon

36 ounces of salmon fillets (this is a fleshy fish so I
calculate that 6 ounces per person will do)
¼ cup olive oil
½ cup chopped green celery leaves
(the younger leaves are best)
½ cup chopped fresh flat-leaf (Italian) parsley
½ cup salted capers (rinsed under running water and
then soaked in bowl of cold water for 30 minutes)
Sea salt and freshly ground black pepper
Juice of 3 lemons
1 lemon, sliced

Olive mixture:

In a small bowl, add olive oil, chopped celery, parsley, and capers. Set aside a spoonful of the chopped
parsley for garnish. Season with salt and pepper.

Salmon:

Place the salmon in an oven platter or shallow
baking pan. Spoon 1/3 of the olive and herb mixture
over the fish. Add lemon juice to the olive and herb
mixture and set aside.

You can bake the salmon with direct heat (in an
oven where the fire has been moved to one side) or
indirect heat (where the embers and fire have been
removed). Bake the salmon in a 450 degree F oven for
15-20 minutes—depending on the size of the fillets.

Remove from the oven and place on a serving
platter. Add the remaining olive mixture to the baking dish and put dish back into the oven for about 1-2
minutes to combine with the fish juices.

Pour the olive sauce over the salmon, sprinkle
the rest of the parsley on top, and serve with a slice
of lemon.

Salmon and marinating sauce ready for grilling in the oven.

Wood-Fired Black Cod and Fennel

SERVES FOUR

1 lb Black Cod filet, cleaned, skin left on one side of fish
1/2 fennel bulb, sliced thin
3 tablespoons of olive oil
1 handful of fresh or dry rosemary
Sea salt and pepper to taste

Mix the olive oil and spices with the sliced fennel. Marinate the fish in this mix of oil and spices for 30 minutes.

Build a fire in your wood-burning oven using dry and split hardwood. When the fire has burned down to coals, you have a choice of either grilling the fish or baking it in a dish.

TO GRILL: Rake a nice bed of hot coals towards the front of your oven and place a freestanding grill over the coals so that they extend about 3" beyond the grill. Wait 5 minutes until the grill is hot, then slide it out and grease it with a clean cloth dipped in olive oil. Place the marinated cod on the grill with the skin side down; it will be done in about 10 minutes.

TO BAKE: If you don't have a freestanding grill, you can use a baking dish. Push the coals and embers to the left or right side of the oven and then wait until the oven temperature registers around 500 degrees F. Place the dish at some distance from the embers. The fish will be done in 10-15 minutes.

Serve with a fresh endive and tomato salad.

VEGETABLES

Eggplant and zucchini are cherished summer staples in Southern Italy, especially when paired with mushrooms and grilled in the oven. With fresh baked bread, they make a great appetizer.

Oven-Grilled Eggplant, Zucchini, and Mushrooms

SERVES SIX

3 medium eggplants, sliced ¾ inch thick lengthwise
6 medium sized zucchini, sliced ¾ inch lengthwise
3 large Portobello mushrooms or a package of cremini mushrooms, sliced ½ inch thick

Marinating sauce:
½ cup virgin olive oil
¼ cup of balsamic red vinegar
Chopped fresh herbs: sage, oregano, thyme, and rosemary
2 garlic cloves, peeled and pressed in a garlic press
Handful of black dried cured olives, chopped
Sea salt and freshly ground black pepper

Slice the eggplants. Place a layer of eggplant in a colander, lightly salting each slice. Continue layering and adding salt on each new layer. Cover with plastic or a plate, place a weight on top and set aside for 30 minutes.

In a small bowl, add olive oil, balsamic vinegar, chopped herbs, chopped olives, pressed garlic, salt, and pepper. Mix this marinating sauce and set aside.

Slice the zucchini and the mushrooms. Place them in a large bowl, add 2 tablespoons of marinating sauce, and gently mix. Cover and set aside.

Take the cover off the eggplant slices. Drain and lightly wash off salt under running water. Pat dry with a towel and place in a large bowl. Add 2 tablespoons of marinating sauce and gently mix. Cover and set aside.

In the oven, spread embers and coals over the middle of the floor and place a freestanding grill on top. After 5 minutes, remove the grill (metal will be very hot so be sure to use gloves). Use metal tongs to set vegetables and mushrooms on the grill, place the grill back in the oven over the embers.

When vegetables are done on one side, turn them using the tongs. When they're finished grilling, place them on a platter and spoon the rest of the marinating sauce on top.

These are the white beans so popular in Tuscany. Beans benefit from baking in a low-temperature oven, becoming creamy and soft in the process. Navy beans can be used if you cannot find the Cannellini.

Below, I list two ways of cooking beans: The slow method is a practical way of using the last bit of heat in the oven. When you are done cooking for the day, put a pot of beans in the oven, close the door, and retrieve a perfectly done bean pot a few hours later.

Baked Cannellini Beans

SERVES SIX

1 ¼ cup dried Cannellini beans
3 cloves of garlic, sliced or whole
Handful of fresh sage leaves, chopped or whole
One pinch of hot pepper flakes
Extra virgin olive oil (6 tablespoons for fast method; 2 tablespoons for slow method)
Sea salt and freshly ground black pepper

Fast method:

Soak the beans overnight.

Drain the beans and place them in a baking dish. Add garlic, sage, and enough water to fill three-quarters of the baking dish. Add 6 tablespoons of olive oil to cover the beans. Cover the dish with foil and make a small hole in the center with the point of a knife to allow steam to escape.

Place the casserole in a 400 degree F wood-fired oven and cook about 45 minutes until they are tender. Cooking time depends on the quality of the beans. The liquid will evaporate and the beans will be nice and soft. Season generously with salt and pepper.

Slow and easy method:

No need to soak the beans overnight.

Wash the beans, place them in a crock-pot, and cover with water (about three parts of water to one part beans). Add olive oil, garlic, sage, and seasoning. Place the lid on the crock-pot or if it doesn't have a lid, use foil and make a small hole in the center to allow steam to escape. Leave in a cooled wood-fired oven (about 350 degrees F) with the door closed for approximately 3-4 hours.

TIP:

You can easily grow oregano, sage, and thyme in a vase or directly in your garden. Use them fresh or harvest and dry. These are great herbs to have around a wood fired oven!

Wood-Fired Tomatoes

SERVES SIX

6 medium tomatoes, ripe but firm
2 russet potatoes
1 cup of olive oil + 2 tablespoons
1/2 cup breadcrumbs
2 teaspoons dry oregano
Salt and pepper to taste

Cube the potatoes and boil them in salted water. When they are done, mash the potatoes with a fork. Set aside.

Cut off the top of the tomato with a sharp knife. Holding the tomato in the cup of your hand, gently scoop out the pulp, making sure not to tear the tomato skin. Keep the pulp and juice for later use.

I like to make my own breadcrumbs from left-over dry baguettes or good Italian bread loaves. Break the hardened bread into larger pieces and process in a food processor, stopping when the mix is still uneven with some crumbs a bit larger than others. Place the breadcrumbs in a bowl and add about 8 tablespoons of the tomato juice and the pulp you had set aside earlier.

Mix in the 2 tablespoons of olive oil, the 2 teaspoons of dry oregano, and salt and pepper to taste. Then add the mashed potatoes and mix. Scoop this mixture into each tomato.

Place the tomatoes snugly either in two loaf pans or other metal pan. Add the olive oil so that it comes up about 1/2 inch. Baste the tomatoes with some of the olive oil.

Slide into the wood-fired oven at the end of your cooking cycle, when the oven has already cooled off to about 300 degrees F. Bake for 20 minutes. Take out and baste the tomatoes with the olive oil in the pan. Return to the oven for another 20 minutes.

DESSERTS

What I love about the following two recipes is that not only are they delicious, but they are also easy to prepare. This allows me to spend more time with my guests while delighting them with a gourmet treat to end the meal.

A gadget called a apple-corer-slicer takes center stage in this first recipe. It elegantly and effortlessly removes the core and slices the apple, making it look great on the serving plate.

Apple slicer, peeler, and corer.

Apples ready to go in the oven.

Apple Delight

FOR EACH INDIVIDUAL APPLE

1 tablespoon butter
3-4 tablespoons of dark brown sugar
¼ cup rum

Core and slice each apple. Arrange the apples snugly, tops up, in a baking dish. Stuff each apple core to its top alternating layers of butter and brown sugar. Pour Rum in the core and over the apple. Prepare next apple in the same fashion.

Place in a 550-500 degree F oven for 20 minutes, remove and baste with rum sauce. Return apples to the oven for 25-30 minutes. Serve with vanilla ice cream or whipped cream.

Summer Dream Peach Cobbler

SERVES 10-12

1 stick of butter (1/2 cup)
1 cup of flour
1 ½ teaspoons baking powder
½ teaspoon salt
1 cup sugar
1 cup milk
3 cups peeled and sliced fresh, good-quality peaches

Courtesy of Henry Parsons.

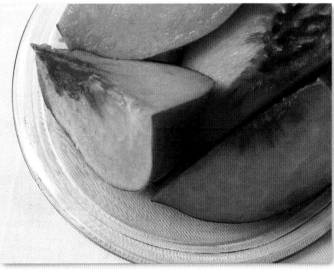

Summer peaches from the farmer's market.

Peel and slice the peaches and set them aside in their juice.

The wood fired oven should be about 350 degrees F. Bake this cobbler with direct or indirect heat.

Put the butter in a 9" x 13" baking dish and place it in the oven. While the butter is melting, mix the flour, baking powder, salt, sugar, and milk in a bowl until it forms a batter.

When the butter has completely melted, remove the pan from the oven and pour the batter into the melted butter. Carefully spoon the peaches and juices over the batter. Return the dish to the oven and bake for about 30-40 minutes. The batter will rise to cover the peaches and the sugar will caramelize making a lovely browned topping. Serve with vanilla ice cream or whipped cream.

Photo by Louis Wang.

This is a great dessert for occasions such as Thanksgiving and Christmas. It can be prepared one day in advance and it has a wonderful creamy flavor that is enhanced when baked in a wood-fired oven.

Wood–Fired Apricot Cheese Cake

SERVES SIXTEEN

2 cups finely crushed butter cookies (about 30 cookies, such as "Lorna Doone")
1/3 cup of butter, melted
1 15 1/4-oz. can unpeeled apricot halves
3 8-oz. pkgs. cream cheese, softened
1 cup caster sugar, regular sugar is ok
1 1/2 tsp. vanilla
3 eggs
1 10-oz. jar of low-calorie apricot spread
1/4 cup apricot nectar

Desserts are baked in the lower temperatures of your pizza oven when you have already cooked other dishes and the oven is at the end of its retained heat cycle. The oven should only have embers in it, brushed to one side, and the floor should register about 360 degrees F.

Crust: Combine crushed cookies and melted butter. Press mixture evenly on bottom and 2 inches up on the sides of a 9-inch metal spring-form pan. Place the pan on the oven floor, close to the opening, for about 5 minutes until it browns, turning it once or twice. Slide out of the oven and set aside.

Filling: Drain apricot halves, reserving 3 tablespoons of the syrup. Coarsely chop the apricots, set aside. In a large mixing bowl beat cream cheese, sugar, the reserved syrup, and vanilla with an electric mixer until combined. Add eggs all at once, beating at low speed until combined. Stir in chopped apricots. Pour filling into crust-lined pan.

Place the pan onto the wood-fired oven floor, close to the opening, and place the oven door on the outside of the arch (so that the opening is not completely sealed, but there's a good air space on top). Check after 10-15 minutes and turn the pan. Check again after 10 minutes and, if you find that the cheesecake is browning too quickly, then place a piece of foil on top of the pan. If needed, add an upturned baking sheet under the pan for extra insulation. The cheesecake will be done in 40 minutes, when the center appears nearly set. If a few small cracks appear on the surface, it is definitely done.

Cool the pan on a wire rack for 15 minutes. Loosen the crust from the sides of the pan and cool the cheesecake for 30 minutes more. Remove the sides of the pan and let the cake cool completely.

Glaze: In a small saucepan combine the apricot nectar and the apricot spread over low heat. Melt while stirring. Remove from heat. Spread over the cheesecake.

Cover and chill the cheesecake in the refrigerator for at least 4 hours before serving or overnight.

CHAPTER EIGHT

PHOTO GALLERY

Building an oven is truly a labor of love, dedicated to creating a space where one can recover from daily worries, relax, and enjoy great food with family and friends. This photo section will provide you with some inspiration and ideas, especially in showcasing the creative use of stone and other materials, as well as the different shapes an oven can take in your garden and in your home. Upon completion of your project, you will most likely feel like you brought home a part of Italy, a small sanctuary of warmth and grace in your backyard.

Old World wood-fired oven in stone and with the flue on the outside. *Photo by Jeff Lewis.*

Housing has been constructed to neatly open up to a small oven. Japan.
Photo by Joe Hashimoto.

Detail. There's simple elegance in the detailed brick lining of this oven. *Photo by Joe Hashimoto.*

Detail. The sun tiles around the arch convey happy memories of good food shared around the table. *Courtesy of Bernice James and Glen Mowrer.*

Opposite: Taking up minimal space in the corner, yet the center of attention, this oven conveys warmth and beauty reminiscent of its Spanish influence. *Courtesy of Bernice James and Glen Mowrer.*

Mediterranean-style oven, painted in warm colors. The perfect
solution for a small space. *Photo by Gigi Meroni.*

The elegant lines of this oven show their practical side by offering plenty of wood storage.
Courtesy of Anthony Walton.

Circular bar counter follows the shape of the pool, allowing a place for guests to sit and chat with the chef. *Courtesy of Gary Rosentrater.*

On the inside of the circular counter there's plenty of room for the chef's work. *Courtesy of Gary Rosentrater.*

Detail.

Shaded under a stately oak in a California vineyard, this oven plays the main role in many parties. *Courtesy of Honea Vineyards.*

A man's best friend: the oven, or the dog? *Courtesy of Honea Vineyards.*

A garden centerpiece surrounded by beautiful rock construction, this large oven easily provides food for a big gathering. *Courtesy of Justin Vineyards & Winery, Inc.*

Sideview. *Courtesy of Justin Vineyards & Winery, Inc.*

95

A grand oven unexpectedly nestled in a stone wall, with plenty of counter space. *Courtesy of Justin Vineyards & Winery, Inc.*

Small, built with great attention to detail, and with plenty of wood to cook with! *Courtesy of Bonnie Nitta and Jack Schrerrer.*

Among the roses and under the blue sky, this oven has been lovingly constructed in stone to last for many years of outdoor cooking. *Courtesy of Nader Ameripour.*

Opposite: Detail of a chimney cap with pizza man weather wane. *Courtesy of Zager Family.*

Oven tucked into a corner of the terrace with a pizza slice mosaic adorning the top. *Courtesy of Andrea and Daniel Schink.*

Detail of mosaic. *Courtesy of Andrea and Daniel Schink.*

A speckled sandstone face makes this oven an attractive corner element for this patio. *Courtesy of Beth Pokorny.*

A work in progress, this outdoor kitchen project shows off vintage tiles on the oven's roof. *Courtesy of Anthony D. Carreon.*

A very creative geometrical solution to storing wood enhances
the sleek lines of an outdoor kitchen setting.

Wood-fired cooking is juxtaposed to the tranquil sound of a
water fountain in this quiet patio sanctuary.

The oven and the fireplace are united in an adobe-style masterpiece
with five albacore shells adorning the front. The stonework on each
arch blends in effortlessly, creating a timeless statement of elegance.

Happiness is a piping hot pizza served poolside! An angel, depicted in Italian tile, guards the chef's work.

A streamlined structure with slanted roof and stucco walls is perfect for cooking outside, under the

Encased in vintage brick construction reminiscent of old times is a modern modular wood-fired oven that will provide many years of gourmet meals.

Guests can gather around under the portico to enjoy the hypnotic power of the fire while the cook bakes pizza and pasta in this stone oven.

Soft curves and white washed walls evoke happy memories of warm Mediterranean evenings spent around the table, chatting and enjoying wood-fired food.

A welcoming cooking corner built in river rock to complement
the beautiful garden wall. It will withstand years of use and deliver
many unforgettable meals.

A classic gable house construction built in Tuscan style, faced with solid stonework and with a generous ledge in granite for the organized chef.

Next to the oven is the ultimate seating area during a warm summer day to leisurely watch the cook and enjoy a drink before the meal without ever leaving the cool waters of the pool.

Reminiscent of ancient castles in the Italian countryside, fireplace and oven are built to last and give an enduring element of elegance to this sunny patio.

Nestled in a fragrant corner of the herb garden under the shade of
a magnolia, a bench provides space for quiet contemplation away
from everyday worries, while waiting for a batch of bread baking
in the oven.

Brick, stucco, and stainless steel set the tone for a fiery oven that will bake countless gourmet meals for large gatherings of friends and family under the blue sky.

The stone patio accommodates stainless steel furniture where guests can enjoy the warm glow of the fire in the oven and the sunset in the distance.

Opposite page: A minimalist take on a wood –fired oven that blends in perfectly with the modern lines of a patio by the beach.

Like a temple of stone dedicated to outdoor living, this oven is
surrounded by counters reflecting the blue open sky and will be
no doubt enjoyed by many grateful guests.

Everyone's attention is riveted towards the focus of the party: a wood-fired oven in stone, surrounded by a circular counter and bar under the shade of a wood trellis. *Courtesy of Sampson and Maureen Brown.*

This structure is pre-assembled, portable and ready to be transported to a welcoming backyard. The white stucco is a perfect contrast for the Italian-style brickwork.

The shape of this oven is reminiscent of a Tuscan farmhouse with its stone roof and large chimney. The granite ledge all around the front underlines the quiet beauty of this outdoor project. *Courtesy of Sal Oliva.*

Detail of the limestone arch and its stylish keystone.

The design takes advantage of a sunny spot in the back of the oven to grow herbs, evoking a windowsill you might find in an Italian village. The cook will not have to go far for some basil or oregano to garnish a pizza pie. *Courtesy of Tracy Newllin Photography.*

A dreamy stucco and stone oven with artistic tiles framing the opening stands in a tranquil spot in the garden. Piping hot pizza after a dip in the pool is the best part of summer!

125

Surrounded by a graceful combination of granite and stone, this pizza oven is the focal point of a shaded outdoor dining area to be enjoyed all year long with family and friends. *Courtesy of Spencer Residence.*

Bold and modern, this oven installation makes good use of the space in the backyard entertainment area to highlight gourmet cooking by the fire. The metal chimney and backsplash have been given a patina finish that complements well with the green background. *Courtesy of Rob Steiner, Landscape Architect.*

This outdoor wood-fired oven is a work of art, each tile carefully selected and the stucco structure highlighted by a custom-made copper chimney pot. There's a place to store the long-handled peels and tools right under the oven.

A true "house of pizza" dedicated to good food, built in stone with a gable roof and a large rounded ledge matching the terracotta arch.

A magical corner of the backyard surrounded by fragrant herbs and cozy nooks to enjoy good food baked in the pizza oven.
Courtesy of Richard Alexander

A fire blazes in the hearth of this outdoor pizza oven handsomely framed
in stone between two solid columns. It
is easy to relax after a dip in the pool
and lounge waiting for gourmet food
to bake in the oven. The fire pit adds a
warm glow late into the evenings. *Courtesy of Tracy Newllin Photography.*

A wood-fired oven set directly into the wall of the house
and faced with rustic stones and Tuscan terracotta bricks.

Not far from the wood-fired oven is a large kitchen area with all the
modern amenities that make outdoor entertainment easy. A large clock
on the wall will make sure the pizza comes out in time!

Stucco paired with sand colored tiles and granite gives an elegant Mediterranean look to this oven under a pergola. When pizza is served, one would think it is all taking place in Sorrento. *Courtesy of Dominic and JoAnna Munafo.*

Perfectly matched to the spacious terrace and elegant residence, the oven brings a touch of Italian romance to the outdoor setting. *Courtesy of Dominic and JoAnna Munafo.*

The absolute centerpiece next to a sparkling pool, this oven provides a great outdoor kitchen to bake a few pizzas or an entire gourmet meal at the end of a pleasant summer day.

An outdoor heater and café style tables come in handy when entertaining outdoors. A pizza oven attracts a lot of friends, so you'd better be ready!

Like a sculpture in the garden nestled between topiaries, this oven stands proud in white with light marble ledges.

Inspired by moss-covered boulders at the edge of the wood, this oven installation has incorporated a natural rock ledge and kept a low profile with a grey stucco finish that follows the curvature of the dome. *Courtesy of Steve Lantner.*

This wood-fired oven has a sleek, casual elegance that spells relaxation, while at the same time providing all the space and tools that a home chef needs when cooking outdoors. *Courtesy of Charles Flewellen.*

An idyllic setting among the roses is a perfect location for this oven; it is faced with bold tile work where blue and terracotta colors highlight an arch whimsically lined with pebbles. You know the food is going to be good! *Courtesy of Michael Manetas.*

The smooth, light stucco finish, the granite counters and arch, the stainless steel and elegant tile work all come together to highlight the timeless style of this fabulous outdoor kitchen. *Courtesy of Charles Flewellen.*

With a stunning view like this, it is no wonder that family and friends want to spend the entire summer outside by the pizza oven enjoying great food and the quiet sounds of nature.

A large outdoor entertainment area by the pool centers on the wood-fired oven with plenty of space to gather under an umbrella or to sit and keep the cook company at the "pizza counter."

Shade around this sunny oven is provided by creatively mixing umbrella trellises and triangular sail shades.

Tuscany has been brought home to the backyard with this oven installation. A wonderful use of stone accentuates the Italian style so beloved not only in cooking dishes but also in building a pizza oven to enjoy for years to come.

This pizza oven's construction in brick would make an Italian mason proud! Built in the shelter of a large patio cover, this outdoor kitchen has all the amenities needed to provide great entertainment all year round. *Courtesy of Michael and Karen Chidiac.*

An up-to-date, streamlined outdoor kitchen mixes Old World culinary traditions with modern technology.

It is a good idea to provide the cooking area with lighting fixtures to extend the use of the outdoor kitchen into the evenings, even though the fire in the oven will give its own warm glow to gatherings.

A lake is the inspiration for this wood-burning oven and plenty of seating is arranged so that guests can enjoy the view. In the meantime, the cook can bake pizzas and roasts out of a beautiful oven faced with round rocks. What a perfect outdoor setting! *Courtesy of Jay and Elisa Arne.*

Children enjoy pizza immensely and love to help garnishing the pizza pies to their own liking. What a great way to inspire baking skills in young talent! *Courtesy of Neal Fossile.*

A splendid indoor wood-fired oven shows off the elegant lines of the detailed masonry and perfectly complements the marble floors. *Courtesy of Neal Fossile.*

139

The arch is solidly framed by precisely laid stonework and the chimney is elegantly set in the middle. This oven is a well-planned addition to an outdoor deck overlooking the garden.

Clever use of this deck includes beautiful stonework surrounding the oven, with matching granite countertops.

A handy wood storage nook has been placed below the oven, away from the deck area.

RESOURCES

ANNA'S BLOG

www.losangelesovenworks.com
This is my blog where I write about wood-fired oven recipes, review oven tools and insulating materials, and where you will find regular up-to-date information about pizza ovens.

THE BREAD BAKERS GUILD OF AMERICA

3203 Maryland Avenue
North Versailles, PA 15137
(412) 823-2080
www.bbga.org
Great resource for bread bakers with many recipes and articles.

CENTRAL MILLING FLOUR

www.centralmilling.com
A wide choice of organic flour, including several pizza and bread mixes. This water-powered mill is nestled by the Logan River and the Rocky Mountains in Utah. Their Type "00 Normal" Flour is very close to the Italian Caputo Flour and designed to take the high temperature of a pizza oven.

HUDSON CREAM FLOUR

P. O. Box 7, Church Street
Hudson, KS 67545
(800) 530-5660
www.hudsoncream.com
This mill produces excellent flour since 1882. Very similar to the European triple O flour and great for pizza and bread baking.

KING ARTHUR CATALOG STORE

135 Route 5 South
Norwich, VT 05055
(800) 827-6836
www.kingarthurflour.com
Supplies and information for the home baker.

LOS ANGELES OVENWORKS

(800) 516-5716
www.losangelesovenworks.com
Importers of Italian modular wood-fired ovens and of pizza oven tools and accessories.

MOLINO CAPUTO FLOUR

www.molinocaputo.it
Antimo Caputo Chef's Flour, the famous type "OO" flour from Italy, with a low gluten content that makes it ideal for stretching the pizza dough. Don't try this flour for pizza baked in your regular gas oven, as it will not brown properly.

NATIONAL CONCRETE MASONRY ASSOCIATION

13750 Sunrise Valley Drive
Herndon, VA 20171-4662
(703) 713-1900
www.ncma.org
Information on concrete and concrete block construction.

NO-KNEAD BREAD RECIPES

www.artisanbreadinfive.com
The book Artisan Bread in Five Minutes a Day by Jeff Hertzberg and Zoe Francois is excellent for teaching you how to bake bread with the no-knead method, saving you a lot of time. Their website has great videos as well.

THE PERLITE INSTITUTE INC.

4305 North Sixth Street Suite A
Harrisburg, PA 17110
(717) 238-9723
Information and resource for perlite.

WHOLE FOODS FLOUR

www.WholeFoods.com
Whole Foods' 365 Organic Unbleached All Purpose Flour is a good choice for home baking if you are just in need of the occasional 1 lb bag. (At the time of printing, Central Milling is providing the flour for this label.)

ENDNOTES

CHAPTER ONE

[1] Pompeii was buried by an eruption of Mt. Vesuvius in 79 A.D. A great number of bakeries (33) have been excavated from the ruins. They are identified by the presence of large wood-burning ovens and stone mills to grind grain.

[2] *Pizzaiolo* is the Italian term for one who is skilled in making pizzas.

[3] Brick ovens are still being built today. It is a longer and more costly process, but a fascinating one. I will refer my readers who would like to know more about how to build a brick oven from scratch to read *The Bread Builders: Hearth Loaves and Masonry Ovens* by Daniel Wing and Alan Scott (White River Junction, VT: Chelsea Green Publishing Company, 1999).

CHAPTER TWO

[1] Calculations are approximate due to variation in oven sizes. Each pizza and loaf of bread is 10 inches in diameter.

CHAPTER THREE

[1] Sardinia is the second largest Italian island after Sicily; its Emerald Coast is of legendary beauty.